STUDIES IN ECONOMIC HISTORY

This new series, specially commissioned by the Economic History Society, focuses attention on the main problems of economic history. Recently there has been a great deal of detailed research and re-interpretation, some of it controversial, but it has remained largely inaccessible to students or buried in academic journals. This series is an attempt to provide a guide to the current interpretations of the key themes of economic history in which advances have recently been made, or in which there has been significant debate.

Each book will survey recent work, indicate the full scope of the particular problem as it has been opened by research and distinguish what conclusions can be drawn in the present state of knowledge. Both old and recent work will be reviewed critically but each book will provide a balanced survey rather than an exposition of the author's own viewpoint.

The series as a whole will give readers access to the best work done, help them to draw their own conclusions in some major fields and, by means of the critical bibliography in each book, guide them in the selection of further reading. The aim is to provide a springboard to further work and not a set of pre-packaged conclusions or short cuts.

STUDIES IN ECONOMIC HISTORY

Edited for the Economic History Society by Professor M. W. Flinn

PUBLISHED

IN PREPARATION

Inflation in Tudor and Early Stuart England

Prepared for
The Economic History Society by

R. B. OUTHWAITE, B.A., PH.D.

*Lecturer in Economic History
at the University of Leicester*

MACMILLAN

First edition 1969
Reprinted 1970

Published by
MACMILLAN AND CO LTD
London and Basingstoke
Associated companies in New York Toronto
Dublin Melbourne Johannesburg and Madras

SBN (paper) 333 10144 8

Printed in Great Britain by
ROBERT MACLEHOSE AND CO LTD
The University Press, Glasgow

HG
937
.O9
1970

Contents

Table

Graph

Acknowledgements

MY objectives have been to trace the emergence and development of the differing opinions about the causes of inflation in Tudor and early Stuart England and to review critically the principal modern interpretations. I have been helped in these tasks by Dr. D. H. Aldcroft and Professor Ralph Davis of Leicester University, Mr. Harland Taylor of Nottingham University, and by the editor of this series, Professor M. W. Flinn, all of whom kindly read drafts of this work. Any virtue the work has owes much to their efforts; for its failings they are held blameless. I am grateful also to Dr. L. A. Clarkson of Queen's College, Belfast, who generously allowed me to read an unpublished paper on the subject of the 'Price Revolution'.

R. B. O.

Leicester
July 1968

Preface

SO long as the study of economic history was confined to only a small group at a few universities, its literature was not prolific and its few specialists had no great problem in keeping abreast of the work of their colleagues. Even in the 1930s there were only two journals devoted exclusively to this field. But the high quality of the work of the economic historians during the inter-war period and the post-war growth in the study of the social sciences sparked off an immense expansion in the study of economic history after the Second World War. There was a great expansion of research and many new journals were launched, some specialising in branches of the subject like transport, business or agricultural history. Most significantly, economic history began to be studied as an aspect of history in its own right in schools. As a consequence, the examining boards began to offer papers in economic history at all levels, while textbooks specifically designed for the school market began to be published.

For those engaged in research and writing this period of rapid expansion of economic history studies has been an exciting, if rather breathless one. For the larger numbers, however, labouring in the outfield of the schools and colleges of further education, the excitement of the explosion of research has been tempered by frustration caused by its vast quantity and, frequently, its controversial character. Nor, it must be admitted, has the ability or willingness of the academic economic historians to generalise and summarise marched in step with their enthusiasm for research.

The greatest problems of interpretation and generalisation have tended to gather round a handful of principal themes in economic history. It is, indeed, a tribute to the sound sense of economic historians that they have continued to dedicate their energies, however inconclusively, to the solution of these key problems. The results of this activity, however, much of it stored away in a wide range of academic journals, have tended to remain inaccessible to many of those currently interested in the subject. Recognising the need for guidance through the burgeoning and confusing literature that has grown around these basic topics, the Economic History Society decided to launch this series of small books. The books are intended to serve as guides to current interpretations in important fields of economic history in which important advances have recently been made, or in which there has recently been some significant debate. Each book aims to survey recent work, to indicate the full scope of the particular problem as it has been opened up by recent scholarship, and to draw such conclusions as seem warranted, given the present state of knowledge and understanding. The authors will often be at pains to point out where, in their view, because of a lack of information or inadequate research, they believe it is premature to attempt to draw firm conclusions. While authors will not hesitate to review recent and older work critically, the books are not intended to serve as vehicles for their own specialist views: the aim is to provide a balanced summary rather than an exposition of the author's own viewpoint. Each book will include a descriptive bibliography.

In this way the series aims to give all those interested in economic history at a serious level access to recent scholarship in some major fields. Above all, the aim is to help the reader to draw his own conclusions, and to guide him in the selection of further reading as a means to this end, rather than to present him with a set of pre-packaged conclusions.

University of Edinburgh
Spring, 1968

M. W. FLINN
General Editor

Some Measures of the Price Rise

WHETHER the inflation experienced by the Tudors and early Stuarts was tantamount to a 'price revolution', the name given to it originally by historians who had yet to experience the startling price rises of the past fifty years,[1] is largely a matter of one's vantage point. It is true that from a mid-twentieth century position the inflationary experience of the Tudors was extremely mild,[2] but at its most rapid, in the middle decades of the sixteenth century, it aroused great concern, especially coming as it did after a century or more of relative price stability. It was also almost certainly more rapid and sustained than anything experienced in England during the early middle ages or the three centuries following the sixteenth. 'The most marked feature,' said Professor Phelps Brown and Miss Hopkins of a graph depicting the movements of certain prices over seven centuries of our history, 'is the extent, and persistence, of the Tudor inflation: what carried it on so far, and why did it end when it did?'[3] To these questions we might add others. What caused it? When did it begin?

In Table I two measures of the price rise are reproduced; both are indexes of current prices, that is the prices which were actually paid or received by consumers and producers, the only prices that mattered to contemporaries. These indexes, like all indexes, were produced for a specific purpose: in this case the original purpose was to try to measure the changing purchasing power of a building operative's money wage. They have, however, been more widely applied, erroneously in theory and perhaps misleadingly in

[1] The phrase appeared first in Georg Wiebe, *Zur Geschichte der Preisrevolution des 16. und 17. Jahrhunderts* (Leipzig, 1895). Wiebe was referring, of course, not solely to England and its inflation but to the price rise in western Europe generally.

[2] This is the view taken by J. D. Gould, 'The Price Revolution Reconsidered', *Economic History Review*, 2nd series, XVII (1964–5), 250.

[3] E. H. Phelps Brown and Sheila V. Hopkins, 'Seven Centuries of the Prices of Consumables, Compared with Builders' Wage-rates', *Economica*, XXIII (1956), 296–314.

9

Table I

Indexes of (1) price of a composite unit of foodstuffs; (2) a sample of industrial products

(1451–75 = 100)

	(1)	(2)		(1)	(2)
1401–10	115	107	1551–60	315	186
1411–20	111	107	1561–70	298	218
1421–30	107	108	1571–80	341	223
1431–40	118	106	1581–90	389	230
1441–50	95	101	1591–1600	530	238
1451–60	98	99	1601–10	527	256
1461–70	105	103	1611–20	583	274
1471–80	93	100	1621–30	585	264
1481–90	121	103	1631–40	687	281
1491–1500	100	97	1641–50	723	306
1501–10	106	98	1651–60	687	327
1511–20	116	102	1661–70	702	343
1521–30	159	110	1671–80	675	351
1531–40	161	110	1681–90	631	310
1541–50	217	127	1691–1700	737	331

practice, to measure changes in the value of money generally.[1] Because they figure so prominently in the only sustained analysis made in recent years of the English price rise, they are reproduced here.[2] This particular series is available only in the form of decade averages, and to provide some idea of the annual fluctuations masked by this form, Fig. I graphs the yearly movements of a

[1] See below, pp. 31–2, where some of the difficulties of producing a general price index, and some of the weaknesses of price materials, are discussed.

[2] Especially the analysis of Mr. Y. S. Brenner. Columns 1 and 2 of Table I are drawn from the table in E. H. Phelps Brown and Sheila V. Hopkins, 'Wage-rates and Prices: Evidence for Population Pressure in the Sixteenth Century,' *Economica*, XXIV (1957), 306. Column 1 is an index of the prices of certain grainstuffs, malt, butter and cheese, and meat and fish, weighted in the proportions 20%, $22\frac{1}{2}$%, $12\frac{1}{2}$% and 25%; column 2 is an unweighted index of a few industrial products: charcoal, candles, oil, some canvas, shirting, woollen cloth, some building materials, and lead and solder. Column 1 is weighted to conform with the supposed outlay of a southern building worker. That it does not completely misrepresent the upward climb of agricultural

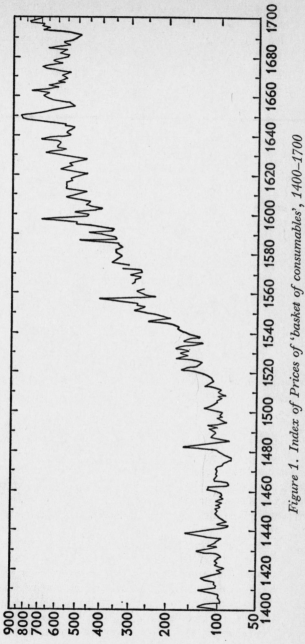

Figure 1. Index of Prices of 'basket of consumables', 1400–1700

composite index, one combining both agricultural and industrial components.[1]

What does this material tell us about the beginning and end of the price rise? There has been a general tendency to push back the beginnings of the rise in current prices. Thorold Rogers, for example, thought that the really decisive break came in the 1540s.[2] It has become currently fashionable, however, to argue that the price rise began much earlier, perhaps around 1480,

---

prices is suggested by comparisons with the index numbers of 'an average of all agricultural products' compiled by P. J. Bowden in his Statistical Appendix to Joan Thirsk (ed.) *The Agrarian History of England and Wales*, vol. IV, *1500–1640* (Cambridge, 1967), p. 862. (Cited hereafter as *AHEW*.)

[1] This is the 'basket of consumables' constructed by E. H. Phelps Brown and Sheila V. Hopkins in their 'Seven Centuries of the Prices of Consumables, compared with Builders' Wage-rates,' *Economica*, XXIII (1956), 296–314. The whole index is weighted to conform with the supposed outlay of a southern building worker. It combines all the items represented in Table I, col. 1, above, as there weighted, with some of the items which figure in col. 2, industrial products (textiles) being given a weight of $12\frac{1}{2}\%$, and fuel and light $7\frac{1}{2}\%$.

[2] J. T. Rogers, *A History of Agriculture and Prices in England*, IV, pp. 727–8 where he comments, 'The most remarkable fact, however, is the period of general low prices which prevails in all products other than those which are merely agricultural from 1490 onwards, for thirty, forty, or even fifty years, as the case may be.' Rogers was inclined perhaps to over-dramatise the break in trend in the '40s since he was determined to prove that it was the debasement of the coinage which produced the marked rise in current prices before Elizabeth's accession. Many of his tables, and the passage cited above, suggest that the break probably came earlier than the 1540s; this is especially true of agricultural prices. Rogers explains this on pp. 736–7: 'I have still to refer to the gradual and steady exaltation of the price of provisions during the last half of Henry the Eighth's reign and before the issue of the base money . . . I account for the rise by the inference that money was slightly cheapened, and was progressively getting cheaper and I think that, had Henry held his hand in 1543, the rise in prices, inevitable from the discovery of the New World, would have gone on the lines and by the degrees indicated in the above figures, though it might have accelerated, as the new silver was rapidly added to the currencies of Europe.'

certainly in the decade after 1510.[1] Table I, which has been used by Mr. Y. S. Brenner to support these statements, would by itself hardly offer strong corroboration. As far as agricultural prices are concerned, for example, it could be argued that it is not until the decade 1521–30 that we get a decided break away from the levels averaged in the previous 120 years. If we look at industrial prices, moreover, the table might suggest an even later break; perhaps the decade beginning 1541, certainly that beginning 1551. Brenner's choices make more sense if we look at the behaviour of the composite index in Fig. I. The major price trough of the year 1477 ends a long period during which prices gently declined, and in the years 1509–22 prices were rising strongly. Using both methods of depicting these figures we can perhaps say that any inflation which took place before 1510 was very gentle, and confined mainly to agricultural prices, and that it was not until the 1520s, when prices failed to descend to the sort of levels which had earlier prevailed, that signs of anything exceptional occurring are evident. It was not until the 1520s also that agricultural wage-rates began to rise, and then only in the immediate vicinity of London. Wage increases elsewhere were delayed until the 1540s and 1550s. Before this agricultural wage-rates had shown a remarkable long-run stability. The same tendencies are revealed in the wages of building operatives: craftsmen's money wages were constant for more than a century before they began to rise in the 1530s; labourers' wages remained virtually unchanged for 130 years before they began to climb in the 1540s.[2]

Once underway, however, inflation proceeded rapidly. This is particularly true of agricultural prices, which reached, by the 1550s, an average level about two and a half times that prevailing 40 years before, and 95 per cent above that of the 1530s. Industrial prices rose more slowly, but even so they were in the 1550s some 70 per cent above those ruling in the 1530s. Agricultural prices moved upwards at a very much more modest pace in the years following 1560,[3] until we reach the 1590s when

[1] Y. S. Brenner, 'The Inflation of Prices in Early Sixteenth Century England', *Economic History Review*, 2nd series, XIV (1961–2), 227.

[2] *AHEW*, p. 864; E. H. Phelps Brown and Sheila V. Hopkins, 'Seven Centuries of Building Wages', *Economica*, XXII (1955), 195–206.

[3] Column 1 of Table I suggests that agricultural prices actually fell in the 1560s below the level of the '50s. Other indexes of agricultural

another great advance occurred. Industrial prices kept pace with agricultural ones from the 1550s to the 1590s, whereas before this they had lagged behind, and they continued their modest advance into the seventeenth century. Apart from a check in the decade 1621–30, their rate of increase was constant but unassuming until the 1670s, when a more stable level of industrial prices began to prevail.[1] As for agricultural prices, the great elevation of the 1590s, when the average level rose by a third, was followed by thirty years of fairly stable prices, until another marked elevation occurred in the 1630s. Agricultural prices rose a little in the 1640s, but from then until the 1690s they fluctuated around a fairly level trend. |

The movements of the composite index in Fig. I, which reflects the behaviour of agricultural prices more than industrial ones, show more clearly the situation with which we have to deal. A sharp upward drive in the second decade of the sixteenth century was followed by more than two decades during which prices fluctuated at a high but stable level. From about the year 1544 to 1551[2] prices rose markedly above previous levels to a new plateau running from then to the early '70s. This was punctuated by sharp increases in the figures for 1556 and 1557, the result of catastrophic harvests in the preceding years 1555–6, and a sharp fall in the 1558 figure, the result possibly of the severe influenza epidemic of 1557.[3] A climb to a slightly higher plateau occurred in the early 1570s, another in the 1590s. Between these periods, however, inflation proceeded very gently. The 1630s marked the ascension to a new higher level after twenty years of very gentle upward drift.

When did the Tudor price rise end? Again recent opinion has

prices show a modest rise. See Bowden's index in *AHEW*, p. 862, where the fall appears to be characteristic only of grain prices.

[1] The overall rate of increase was around only 3 per cent per decade from the 1560s to the '90s, perhaps double this thereafter.

[2] Confusions over dating will arise unless it is remembered that Phelps Brown and Hopkins date the year from the preceding Michaelmas (29 Sept.) to the next, so that their figure for 1545, for example, covers the period from September 1544 to September 1545. In Dr. Bowden's tables however, 1545 refers to the period September 1545 to September 1546.

[3] See F. J. Fisher, 'Influenza and Inflation in Tudor England', *Economic History Review*, 2nd series, XVIII, No. 1 (1965), 120–9.

tended to diverge from earlier views and has been inclined to argue that inflation came to an end in the 1630s. Although some sort of case can be made out for this date if we look at the agricultural prices in Table I, and at Fig. I which tends to be dominated by agricultural products, industrial prices did not begin to level out until the 1670s. It is conceivable that another composite index, one that gives a much greater weighting to industrial prices, would prolong the price rise, produce a generally slower rate of ascension in the Tudor period, and iron out some of the sharp discontinuities.

Bearing these measures, and this chronology of the price rise, in mind let us turn briefly to what contemporaries thought were its causes.

Contemporary Opinions

CONTEMPORARY discussion of the Tudor–Stuart inflation, like much recent analysis of the problem, was coloured by the behaviour of agricultural rather than industrial prices. Dearth, to men at that time, meant usually the high cost of provisions, and in analysing what they thought about dearth and its causes we run into a number of related problems, all of which stem from the highly unstable nature of agricultural product prices. It is often very difficult to discover whether they were referring to short-run oscillations, and especially to the violent upward fluctuations that were likely to result from a series of deficient harvests, or to the longer-run trend, to the general upward drift of prices from one generation to the next. The ambiguity is heightened by the fact that it was usually the short-run situation, a series of deficient harvests, that provoked comment about more general trends in price behaviour. Finally, although some observers were prepared to put forward different reasons to account for the trend as distinct from the fluctuations of prices, others were confused and were led into providing explanations of the trend which were really more suitable for explaining short-term fluctuations.

It is difficult, as a result, to state precisely when contemporaries first became aware of the inflationary trend. There is some discussion of dearth in the early sixteenth century[1] but much of it was probably prompted by preceding harvest failures. There is less ambiguity about the reference in 'An Act Concerning Farms and Sheep' of 1533–4[2] which spoke of the doubling of the price of many basic commodities within recent memory. It was, however, the period 1548–56 which produced by far the greatest volume of comment upon the subject. Before 1548 there was comparatively little notice taken of inflation, and most of that did little more than invoke traditional short-run explanations to account for the experience. After 1556 comment again becomes sporadic, though probably less so than before 1548, but it becomes much more sophisticated. This sophistication owed much, as might be expected, to the differing but severe inflationary experiences of the years 1544–56,[3] and the fierce controversy they engendered. From the 1560s to the early '90s men had, then, comparatively little to say about inflation, a fact which is surely linked with the relative stability of prices in these years. The bad harvests and enormous price fluctuations of the years 1594–7 produced more backward glances, but thereafter comparatively little notice was taken of the subject, and as we move into the seventeenth century parliamentary opinion, at least, became as concerned with the horrors of plenty as it was with the spectre of dearth.[4] It was, therefore, only in the period 1548–56 and, to a lesser extent, the 1590s, that contemporaries became much alarmed about high prices, and it is from the earlier of these two periods that most of the literary comment derives.

Attention was focused mostly upon food prices – upon the dearth of victuals – and some of the earliest explanations, and certainly the most characteristic of the first half of the sixteenth century, were those which laid the blame for high food prices

[1] See, for example, 'An Act Avoiding Pulling Down of Towns', 1515 (7 Hen. VIII, c. 1); in A. E. Bland, P. A. Brown and R. H. Tawney, *English Economic History: Select Documents* (London, 1920), pp. 260–2.

[2] 25 Hen. VIII, c. 13; in Bland, Brown and Tawney, *op. cit.*, pp. 264–6; and *English Historical Documents*, vol. V, *1485–1558*, ed. C. H. Williams (London, 1967), pp. 927–8.

[3] See Fig. I and pp. 13–14 above.

[4] Facets of this are discussed in M. W. Beresford, 'Habitation Versus Improvement; The Debate on Enclosures by Agreement', in F. J. Fisher (ed.), *Essays in the Economic and Social History of Tudor and Stuart England* (Cambridge, 1961), pp. 40–69.

16

upon enclosure, using this term in the wide sense in which it was generally employed by moralists to cover activities as varied as the growth of sheep flocks at the expense of tillage, the engrossing of holdings, the depopulation of villages, and the abrogation of common rights. There can be little doubt that the debates over enclosure were prompted more by the upward movements of grain prices than by any quickening in the incidence of enclosure itself. Apart from the Acts of 1515 and 1533–4 already mentioned, this sort of explanation was very characteristic of the mid-century Commonwealth school.[1] It lost its momentum in the second half of the sixteenth century, but regained some of it during those grain price fluctuations of enormous amplitude which characterised the 1590s. By this time, however, as the speeches on enclosure in the Parliaments of 1597 and 1601 make plain, there were as many fears expressed over the possibility of low prices as there were over high ones.

In the decade and a half following 1544 another very characteristic type of explanation emerges, namely that high prices were the result of the successive debasements and enhancements to which the coinage was then being subjected.[2] This was the trump card of the Doctor in the *Discourse of the Common Weal* (and its author), the theme of powerful sermons by Latimer, and the subject of scholarly treatises on the coinage.[3] It became also

[1] See especially 'The defence of John Hales . . .', printed in E. Lamond (ed.), *A Discourse of the Common Weal of this Realm of England* (Cambridge, 1893), p. lxiv. See also 'Policies to reduce this realme of Englande unto a prosperus wealthe and estate', 1549, printed in R. H. Tawney and E. Power, *Tudor Economic Documents* (3 vols., London, 1924), III, 319, and 'The Decaye of England Only by the Great Multitude of Shepe', 1550–3, *ibid.*, III, 51–2. The most intelligent contemporary appraisal of the role of enclosure in the price rise is to be found in *A Discourse of the Common Weal*, written probably by Sir Thomas Smith in the summer of 1549 (see Mary Dewar, 'The Authorship of the "Discourse of the Commonweal",' *Economic History Review*, 2nd series, XIX (1966), 388–400), especially pp. 15–20 in the Lamond edition.

[2] This was sometimes linked with the previous type of explanation, as by William Lane writing to William Cecil in 1551; see Tawney and Power, *op. cit.*, II, 182–6.

[3] Lamond, *op. cit.*, p. 69; Tawney and Power, *op. cit.*, II, 181; W. A. J. Archbold, 'A Manuscript Treatise on the Coinage written by John Pryse in 1553', *English Historical Review*, XIII (1898), 710.

virtually the official explanation of inflation by the opening of Elizabeth's reign.[1] This type of argument, linking dearth with the deterioration in the precious metal content of money of account,[2] flourished vigorously as might be expected in the period of the great debasement of Henry VIII and Edward VI, and languished with Elizabeth's revaluation of the coinage in 1560–1. The same is true to some extent of the next type of argument.

The decline in the intrinsic value (i.e. precious-metal content) of money of account naturally affected the basic determinant of the foreign exchange rate, the mint par of exchange, and, to cite the most important example, the rate between London and Antwerp plummeted from around 26s. 8d. Flemish to the pound sterling before the great debasement of the 1540s to 13s. 4d. in 1551.[3] At the same time, of course, prices were rising internally. Contemporaries were aware of these simultaneous occurrences, though the precise relationships, and the order of causation, sometimes escaped them. Thus contemporaries frequently argued that the fall of the exchange rate was, as William Lane put it in 1551, 'the father of all darthe of allmoste alle thynges that man occapyythe.'[4]

Other explanations, equally ephemeral though not as intimately linked with these monetary events of the mid-century, include thorough discussion of factors causing limitations of supply. Mention has been made already of the fact that contemporaries were liable to fall back upon explanations which were often more suited to explain short-term than long-term price

[1] See especially the memorandum of 1559 on the reasons for the reform of the coinage and the proclamation of September 1560 announcing the reform: Tawney and Power, *op. cit.*, II, 193, 196.

[2] See below, p. 25, note 1, where 'money of account' is explained.

[3] This is explained most clearly in G. Unwin's essay, 'The Merchant Adventurers' Company in the Reign of Elizabeth', in R. H. Tawney (ed.), *Studies in Economic History: The Collected Papers of George Unwin* (London, 1927), pp. 154–7.

[4] Tawney and Power, *op. cit.*, II, 183; see also 'Policies to reduce this realme of Englande . . .' of 1549, *ibid.*, III, 315–8; and the memorandum prepared in 1564 for the royal commission on the exchanges, *ibid.*, III, 346–59, which argues that price levels were determined basically by the rate of exchange.

fluctuations. Quite frequently, therefore, price rises are explained in terms of increasing speculation[1] and the accursed activities of middlemen.[2] Poor harvests, if they produced little else, brought forth abundant crops of such complaints. Monopolies came under the lash from the 1580s onwards.[3]

Increasing demands figured almost as largely as limitations on supply in sixteenth-century explorations of the causes of dearth. Government demands were said at various times to be excessive or otherwise oppressive.[4] Such accusations were sometimes levelled at the Crown's normal rights of provision (purveyance), more often when demands were swollen by vigorous military campaigning. Exports also received a certain amount of blame. An Act of 1555 castigated those 'covetous and unsatiable persons seking their onely lucers and gaynes' who were exporting provisions etc., 'By reason wherof, the sayd Corne Vyctuall and Wood arre growen unto a wonderfull dearthe and extreame pryses.'[5] The Act went on to fix the prices below which it was not an offence to export provisions, a ceiling which tended to advance in the century which followed.[6] Every poor harvest tended, however, to produce its crop of fears about excessive exportation.

[1] See the proclamations of 1545 and 1586 (printed in Bland, Brown and Tawney, *op. cit.*, pp. 367–9, 374–80). These accusations owed much to the prevalence of bad harvests – those of both years being amongst the poorest of the century – and not a little also to heavy government demands for soldiers' provisions. On this last point see the interesting discussion of the 'Book of Orders' of 1587 in Brian Pearce, 'Elizabethan Food Policy and the Armed Forces', *Economic History Review*, XII (1942), 39–46; and C. S. L. Davies, 'Provisions for Armies, 1509–50. A Study in the Effectiveness of Early Tudor Government', *ibid.*, 2nd series, XVII (1964), 234–48.

[2] See John Hales (?) in 1549 (Tawney and Power, *op. cit.*, II, 219); Thomas Lever, 1550 (*ibid.*, III, 49–50); William Harrison in the 1580s (F. J. Furnivall (ed.), *Harrison's Description of England* (London, 1877), p. 300; and Tawney and Power, *op. cit.*, III, 78.

[3] See especially the 'Discourse of Corporations', written in the late 1580s; printed in Tawney and Power, *op. cit.*, III, 265–76.

[4] *Ibid.*, II, 219.

[5] An Act to Restrain Carrying of Corn, Victuals and Wood over the Sea, 1 and 2 Ph. and Mary, c. 5, printed in Tawney and Power, *op. cit.*, I, 150–2.

[6] Fisher, 'Influenza and Inflation in Tudor England', contains an interesting discussion of these and related points.

More interesting to present-day analysts are those very occasional observations as to the possibility that demands were growing because of a rising population. Alderman Box put before Lord Burghley in 1576 a proposal to cultivate waste grounds, and provided a panorama of the previous three centuries when he recounted, 'Ther is a sayinge, and I thincke it trewe, that thes wastes that nowe be came firste by decaye or lacke of people, so that corne and other victuall grewe to be so good cheape, that they dyd suffer their plowes to decaye and their grounde lye waste [rather] then to plowe their grounde and sell their corne and other victuall, so cheap as it was then.' Of this, Professor Postan would no doubt heartily approve.[1] Box continued, moreover, 'But nowe the tyme is alterid, and is otherwise to be considerid. For the people are increassid and grounde for plowes dothe wante, Corne and all other victuall is scante, many straingers sufferid hear, which make the corne and victuall deare. People woulde laboure yf they knew wher one, The husbande man woulde be glade to have grounde to set his plowe to worke yf he knew wher.'[2] Many contemporaries were aware, particularly by the later Elizabethan period, that the population was growing,[3] that pressure upon land was increasing, but few related this to the price rise in quite so explicit a manner as Alderman Box.

Nevertheless, other, what we might term 'physical', explanations of the price rise were not wanting. Outstanding amongst these were those which sought to explain increases in the prices of commodities generally by reference to the prices of particular commodities,[4] and sought to explain price increases in the latter in terms of shifts in supply and demand and by rising costs. The high price of tin was accounted for in 1595, for example, by the tendency for European production to abate in the face of generally increasing demands, 'which scarcetye must necessarely encreasse the price.' And if anyone should still think that the price was likely to fall, the writer added, 'There be also other reasons to

[1] See in particular his 'Some Economic Evidence of Declining Population in the Later Middle Ages', *Economic History Review*, 2nd series, II (1950), 221–46.

[2] Tawney and Power, *op. cit.*, I, 74.

[3] See Fisher, 'Influenza and Inflation', *op. cit.*, *passim*.

[4] This is an important feature of all 'real' or 'physical' explanations as we shall see later.

mayntayne the good price of tyn, as the great derth of corne, and all other provisions, the derth of Tymber to bynde the mynes from fallinge, and of woods to make coles for meltinge the tyn, also ther chardges encreaseth muche by drawinge the water yerlye deper, and of greater quantytye from the bottome of the mynes . . .'[1] The highly interesting 'Policies . . .' of 1549 elicited particular reasons to explain the high price of victuals and of wool, and then proceeded to argue, 'Seinge then that woll is Deare: Clothe muste nedes rise of price accordinglie. And what thinge can be chepe when victuall and Cloth is Deare? Surely nothinge that is wroughte or made by mans hande or laboure: for victuall and Clothe be the most principall things . . .'[2] The *Discourse of the Common Weal* is also full of passages indicating the author's awareness of the interrelated, circular nature of economic activity and the ways in which rising costs could inflate the general price level.

Men of the mid-sixteenth century were puzzled by the price rise, a conclusion which is not incompatible with the firm voice with which they pronounced on both causes and remedies, and a common reaction in such circumstances was to put the whole thing down to human avarice and the tendency for one class to oppress another. The price rise enormously exacerbated sectional disputes. Nowhere is this better mirrored than in the *Discourse of the Common Weal*, and especially interesting, in view of what we have been saying about rising cost explanations, is that section dealing with the rise in rents.[3] There can be little doubt that the *Discourse* reflected much current debate, that men turned upon each other in their efforts to account for something that was not always clearly understood.

Among the least typical of Tudor explanations, although they had a much greater vogue in the seventeenth century, were those which linked inflation with the inflow into Europe of gold and silver from the New World. As far as we know the first English writer to suggest such a link was the author of the *Discourse of the Common Weal*. The passage in which he does so was not in the original version of the treatise, written in 1549, but was inserted later, before its publication in 1581. This strengthens considerably the view that the author of both the original treatise and

[1] Tawney and Power, *op. cit.*, I, 285.
[2] *Ibid.*, III, 320–1.
[3] Lamond, *op. cit.*, pp. 38–9.

21

the inserted passage was in fact the scholarly Sir Thomas Smith, one time ambassador to Paris and monetary enthusiast, who almost certainly would have become aware of the theories of Jean Bodin, the French philosopher and monetary expert, who is often thought of as the first writer to have definitely suggested a link between the specie arriving from the New World and European inflation. Bodin first published his views in 1568, long after the *Discourse* was originally written, but some eight years before Sir Thomas Smith, virtually the English Bodin, sat down to revise some of his earlier writings.[1] The passage is well known but worth repeating. The Doctor had gone to great pains to establish that the prime cause of the rise in prices was the debasement of the coinage, and this was almost certainly Smith's original view. The Knight, in the newly inserted passage, then asks why, if this was the chief cause, had not prices fallen back to their old level with the re-establishment of the coinage in 1561 at its 'former purity and perfection'. The Doctor, after some hesitation, hazards two reasons why prices had not fallen. One was 'this rackynge and hoyssing up of Rentes', producing cost inflation, a process which was still going on. The other was 'the great store and plenty of treasure, which is walking in these partes of the world, far more in these our dayes, than ever our forefathers have sene in times past. Who doth not understand,' the Doctor continued, 'of the infinite sums of gold and silver, which are gathered from the Indies and other countries, and so yearly transported unto these costes?'[2] As was the case in France with Bodin's own work, these

[1] Dewar, *op. cit.*, pp. 398–9. Whether Bodin deserves the accolade of being the originator of the idea, we do not know. He claimed originality, but very brief statements of the idea had appeared in earlier writings, notably Noel du Fail's *Balivernes et contes d'Eutrapel* (1548) and Gomara's *Annals of the Emperor Charles V* (1557). It is unlikely that Bodin knew the latter work, however, and he certainly deserves credit for being the first writer to propound the view in an expanded form. See A. E. Munroe, *Monetary Theory before Adam Smith* (1923; re-printed New York, 1966), p. 56; E. J. Hamilton, 'American Treasure and Andalusian Prices, 1503–1660', *Journal of Economic and Business History*, I (1928), 33. The best discussion of Bodin's views, the spread of his ideas, etc., is the introduction to H. Hauser (ed.), *La Response de Jean Bodin à M. de Malestroit, 1568* (Paris, 1932), which prints Bodin's original statement on this subject.

[2] Lamond, *op. cit.*, pp. 186–7.

22

views had comparatively little impact on contemporaries, not at least before the turn of the century when interest in England was revived by Gerard de Malynes.[1]

How then can we sum up contemporary explanations? Like all which followed, including those of our own day, they were concerned primarily with agricultural prices, for these underwent the greatest rise. Their explanations comprised a mixture of monetary and real or physical elements. The most characteristic monetary explanations were debasement and exchange depreciation, but these were prominent only during the 'great debasement' period. Once this had ended real or physical explanations tended to predominate. The idea that inflation was caused by an influx of New World silver hardly affected English thinking before the end of the sixteenth century. From the seventeenth century onwards, however, monetary elements, and especially New World silver, came to be thought of as the most important causes of inflation. Physical explanations lapsed into unimportance. More recently, however, this situation has tended to be reversed.

We must turn, therefore, to these two different types of explanation, the monetary and the real, and finally suggest briefly how a synthesis might be managed.

Monetary Explanations

THE most important influence for many years on modern English writing about the Tudor and early Stuart inflation was the great Victorian scholar, J. E. Thorold Rogers, who spent his

[1] See Gerard de Malynes, *A Treatise of the Canker of England's Commonwealth* (1601); *England's view, in the unmasking of two paradoxes; with a replication unto the answer of Maister John Bodine* (London, 1603). See also the selections from the 1601 treatise in Tawney and Power, *op. cit.*, III, 386–404, esp. p. 387, 'According to the plentie or scarcitie of the monie then, generally things became dearer or good cheape, whereunto the great store or abundance of monie and bullion, which of late years is come from the West Indies into Christendom, hath made every thing dearer according to the increase of monie . . .' This is pure Bodin.

life collecting and processing price materials stretching from the thirteenth to the nineteenth centuries.[1] On the whole Rogers had little new to say about the causes of the price rise – it was due first of all to debasement and then subsequently to Spanish-American bullion – but the weight of those seven volumes was sufficient to propel this already current orthodoxy well into the twentieth century.[2] All the most important writings on English economic history duly leaned this way, though there was a gradually growing volume of minor criticisms and amendments. Cunningham and Lipson – to cite two of the most influential – did little more than fill out this dual-cause monetary explanation. From the late 1920s a new figure entered the ranks, the American historian, Earl J. Hamilton, who began to produce his work on Spanish price history, work which related intimately the rise in Spanish prices to the influx into Spain of New World treasure.[3] His importance lay not in suggesting such a connection, but in his methods, which owed much to earlier writers such as Wiebe and to the American economist, Irving Fisher. Wiebe was the first writer to attempt to measure systematically and comparatively changes in silver prices, meaning the silver-content prices of money of account, as the best way of establishing whether there were changes in the respective exchange values of precious metals

[1] *A History of Agriculture and Prices in England* (7 vols., Oxford, 1866–1900).

[2] Close reading of Rogers, however, reveals sometimes alarming shifts in emphasis from one of these factors to another. The whole of volume IV for example, which covers the period 1401–1582, is directed towards the assertion that inflation was the direct result of meddling with the coinage. In volume V, published five years later, which deals with the period 1583–1702, he is inclined like the Doctor in the *Discourse* to invoke Spanish bullion to explain the continuation of inflation. Yet he could still say (V, 780) 'as far as the evidence goes which has come before me, there was no change in real prices, that is the proportion which prices of commodities bore to given weights of coin during the greater part, perhaps the whole, of the sixteenth century.' While later (p. 788) he puts forward a view of post-1580 inflation involving cheaper silver, increasing population, etc. Of all his many virtues, re-reading and rigorous self-criticism were conspicuously absent.

[3] Especially his 'American Treasure and Andalusian Prices, 1503–1660', *Journal of Economic and Business History*, I (1928), 1–35.

and commodities.[1] Fisher was the chief refiner of the quantity theory of money; the producer of an equation that has exercised great influence, especially over economic historians.[2] Hamilton's work had less influence in England on discussions about the causes of the price rise than it had on the relationships between that phenomenon and 'capitalist' development.[3] He did, however, bring a new sophistication to discussions of the 'price revolution' generally, and his work became influential, principally on its own merits, but partly also because it received J. M. Keynes' approval in a rather quixotic excursion into history in *A Treatise on Money* (1930).[4] Meanwhile the work of three separate numismatic and financial historians – Oman, Feavearyear and Brooke – perpetuated, predictably enough, an exclusively monetary interpretation of the Tudor-Stuart inflation.[5] At the same time, however, systematic, co-ordinated work was being started, largely under the auspices of the International Scientific Committee on Price History set up by William Beveridge and the American economic historian, E. F. Gay,[6] and important work was also being undertaken independently, notably by European scholars. The results of these efforts, the publication of which was enormously handicapped by later political events, eventually

[1] Money of account here means the accounting units in which prices were normally expressed, that is pounds, shillings and pence in England; livres, sols or sous, and deniers in France, and so on. There was a general historical tendency for the actual weight of silver (and/or gold) in such units to decline. Many writers have thought it necessary, therefore, to recalculate prices according to the actual amount of precious metal contained in the coinage at any one particular time. This was especially the case if the object was to establish whether there was any changing relationship between precious metals and goods. Such recalculated prices are generally referred to as 'silver prices' but are here referred to by the less ambiguous term 'silver-content prices'.

[2] I. Fisher, *The Purchasing Power of Money* (New York, 1911).

[3] Sparked off by his 'American Treasure and the Rise of Capitalism (1500–1700)', *Economica*, IX (1929), 338–57.

[4] 2 vols., London.

[5] C. Oman, *The Coinage of England* (Oxford, 1931); A. Feavearyear, *The Pound Sterling* (Oxford, 1931); and G. C. Brooke, *English Coins* (London, 1932).

[6] The Committee met for the first time in 1930. See Sir W. Beveridge, *Prices and Wages in England* (London, 1930), p. 1.

profoundly modified historians' views. In England, however, right down to the early 1950s, and in print at least, the classic views about causation prevailed, although reservations were being expressed in other media. Sir John Clapham, for example, never usually the most servile to accepted opinion, cast his explanation almost exclusively in monetary terms,[1] along the lines laid down by Rogers, Wiebe and Hamilton. The inflation was the almost accidental result of largely autonomous monetary happenings – debasement and the discovery of New World treasure. Only since the mid-'50s has anything like a sustained reaction set in. It is time now to examine the monetary explanation in some detail, and then to turn to some of the objections that have been levelled against it.

The monetary explanation is usually cast in the form of the quantity theory of money, which argues that the value of money is inversely proportional to the quantity in circulation. This notion was developed from the late Middle Ages onwards, and some implicit recognition of the theory long lay behind explanations of the Tudor price rise. But modern analysts have shown a fondness for more explicit accounts, based often on some variant of Irving Fisher's 'equation of exchange'. The equation is a truism, the result of looking in two different ways at the sum total of transactions taking place in any community over a given period of time, and is represented in its simplest form by the equation $MV = PT$. M represents the total amount of money in circulation, V its rate of turnover, or velocity of circulation, P the average level of prices of all goods traded for money, and T the total volume of transactions, or trade.[2] Fisher himself upheld the pure form of the quantity theory, arguing that changes in M would have little or no effect on V or T and would thus induce proportional changes in P, the level of prices. This did not rule out, however, independent changes in V or T, though these changes, he insists repeatedly, would be independent of initial changes in M. The price level is determined, therefore, by the relative movements in all other variables, thus

$$P = \frac{MV}{T}$$

---

[1] Sir J. Clapham, *A Concise Economic History of Britain* (Cambridge, 1949), pp. 185–7.

[2] Fisher, *op. cit.*, especially chapter II.

but the most likely effect of a movement in M is a proportional change in P.[1]

Hamilton repeatedly makes use of these notions, though not always explicitly, nor does he always accept the logical challenges of the equation.[2] Thus, prices rose in Spain during the sixteenth and early seventeenth centuries primarily because of increases in M. The latter was derived from the great increases in private and public treasure imports into Spain from the New World. Graphs were drawn showing an apparently close similarity between these imports (M) and an index of the average yearly prices expressed in silver currency of some two dozen commodities, representing P. When M began to decline in the early seventeenth century, so also did P. By this time, however, the general level of P was some five times higher than at the beginning of the sixteenth century. Increases in P, however, were not due solely to increases in M, but were also due to decreases in T, to the growing debility of the Spanish economy from the late sixteenth century onwards. Though prices expressed in silver stagnated in the first half of the seventeenth century, current prices continued to rise. This is accounted for by further increases in M (this time due to silver and 'vellon' debasement and the over-issue of vellon[3] and by further decreases in T, increasing economic decadence.[4] Although most of Hamilton's attention was focused upon Spain, he produced evidence, drawn almost entirely from Wiebe, of a later and lesser rise in silver-content prices in England, France and Germany.[5] This, he suggested, was the result of the diffusion of

[1] *Ibid.*, chapter VIII, and especially pp. 156–8.

[2] The 'profit inflation' thesis, for example, is itself a contradiction of the Fisher 'pure form', for an increasing M can seemingly induce changes in T. I must thank Dr. L. A. Clarkson for bringing this point to my attention.

[3] Vellon was coin made initially from a mixture of silver and copper, which by degrees of debasement became pure copper.

[4] This is a bald summary of the ideas contained in the articles in the *Journal of Econ. and Bus. History* (1928) and *Economica* (1929), amplified by his 'Monetary Inflation in Castile, 1598–1660', *Economic History*, II (1930–3), 177–212. The results of all this work were incorporated with certain modifications in his *American Treasure and the Price Revolution in Spain, 1501–1650* (Cambridge, Mass., 1934).

[5] *Journal of Econ. and Bus. History* (1928), pp. 31–3.

New World silver via Spain, and he suggested some of the ways in which such a diffusion took place.[1]

Since Hamilton wrote attempts have been made to apply the Fisher equation to England, and it is with these that we must be primarily concerned. At first it was enough simply to argue that the increase in prices (P) was the direct outcome of increases in the quantity of money (M), brought about mainly through debasements and enhancement of the coinage in the first half of the sixteenth century, accompanied and followed by the inflow of New World bullion. More recently, however, writers have stressed the importance of movements in variables other than M, in V and T. The most notable of these is Mr. Y. S. Brenner. According to his view,[2] 'The rise in prices in England during the first half of the sixteenth century was due to the concatenation of an increasing velocity and volume of currency circulation with a relatively decreased supply of and intensified tightness of demand for agricultural products,' and the same appears to be true of the later price rise. Increases in M were brought about by (i) an increase in the volume and value of coin in circulation and (ii) the relaxation of the usury laws and partial legalisation of various sorts of bills of sale and exchange. The origins of the first of these

[1] This is done mainly in the article in *Economica* (1929), pp. 345–7. This aspect of the subject was always very slightly treated in the Hamilton corpus, since his main concern was with Spanish prices. Briefly, however, he suggests that treasure left Spain through (i) adverse trade balances – the result of Spanish prices rising faster than those of other countries, (ii) divergent bi-metallic ratios, and (iii) payments for Spanish armies in France and the Low Countries. In addition, some treasure was carried directly from the New World possessions by interlopers, and some was intercepted by privateers. These were no more than suggestions; little was offered in the way of corroborative evidence.

[2] As expressed in 'The Inflation of Prices in Early Sixteenth Century England', *Economic History Review*, 2nd series, XIV (1961–2), 225–239; and 'The Inflation of Prices in England, 1551–1650', *ibid.*, XV (1962–3), 266–84. Less important is 'The Price Revolution Reconsidered: A Reply', *ibid.*, XVIII (1965), 392–6. It is often difficult to disentangle Brenner's own views from those of the authorities he is bent on challenging. The clearest account of his own views is probably to be found in the summary of his thesis 'Prices and Wages in England, 1450–1550' in *Bulletin of the Institute of Historical Research*, XXXIV (1961), 103–5, from which most of the quotations in the text come.

factors were diverse: 'successive issues of base and forged coins' in the first half of the sixteenth century, along with 'some easement of the shortage of precious metals'. In the post-1550 period it is due to rising Mint output, the precious metals for which came from reminting old coins already circulating and from the de-hoarding of precious metals cached either as coin or plate. As for Spanish silver, it appears to have played little or no part before 1630 and a very limited one thereafter. Increases in the velocity of circulation were brought about by 'the development of industry and the expansion of commerce, by the sharp rise in speculation in land and on the legalised market for money and by the transition of greater sections of society from a state of rural self-sufficiency into urbanised communities dependent for their supplies on markets.' As for the third determinant of the level of prices, T, we are told: 'The relatively decreased supply of foodstuffs was caused by increased demand due to population growth, exportation, and the shifting of agents of production from employments with only marginal returns to sectors of the economy which temporarily yielded high profits.' Although Mr. Brenner employs the Fisher equation, his analysis does not always fit happily into it. The equation demands that T be judged in relation to MV; we get a great deal of discussion of a 'relatively reduced' T, but it is judged not in relation to MV but with reference to population growth. The relevance of this needs to be questioned.

The Fisher equation obviously still exercises a great fascination over economic historians, though economists have long questioned its value. As stated by Fisher the theory was obviously a truism, but difficulties arise, first, when the assumptions on which the theory is based are questionable (and this is where many economists have taken it to task), and secondly, when attempts are made to apply it to actual historical situations. It is with this latter category of difficulties that we must be chiefly concerned.[1]

M, in the Fisher scheme, is supposed to represent the actual amount of money in circulation. But what do we know of this in

---

[1] The sections which follow owe a great deal to I. Hammarström, 'The "Price Revolution" of the Sixteenth Century: Some Swedish Evidence,' *Scandinavian Economic History Review*, V (1957), 118–54, an article which is much more wide-ranging than its title implies and constitutes the best modern discussion of the 'price revolution' and the problems associated with it.

sixteenth century England? The most important form of money was actual gold and silver coin of the realm, and attempts to assess movements in its quantity are based usually on figures of Mint output. These need to be analysed with a much greater degree of care than anyone has yet exercised, for the simple fact is that Mint output is not the same as additions to the total stock of coin. Secondly, the total stock of coin in use comprised not only English coins but foreign ones as well (including Scottish coins in the border counties). The merchant community was well used to handling French, Spanish, German and Low Country coins, and many of these were virtually legal tender in that the rates at which they should pass were published. Needless to say, we know very little about the circulation of such coins, even whether it increased or decreased in this period. Similar sorts of difficulties arise when we get around to thinking of money other than actual coin, although the number of instruments which fulfilled the functions of money were extremely limited before the mid-seventeenth century. The growing use of bills of exchange, inland bills, and other securities, sometimes cited in support of a growing M is evidence of doubtful validity, since it is arguable that only if such securities are discountable and negotiable can they be stretched so as to fit into the category of money. They had much more important effects on the velocity of circulation than they had on the quantity of money. Even without taking into account such virtually unknown factors as external losses, the extent of hoarding, wear and tear, and counterfeiting, we can safely assert that it is impossible to measure accurately increases in M in the sixteenth and seventeenth centuries. The best we can do is to hazard, supported by intelligent reasoning, that it probably increased. Most accounts, however, ignore many of these difficulties.

If in fact we cannot accurately quantify M, then we cannot even proceed to quantify V, the velocity of its circulation. We can reason that it must have increased, though whether it increased more or less than M is difficult to say. Something better needs to be offered in the way of evidence supporting an increase in V, however, than Brenner's statement that it can be found in increased complaints about middlemen.[1]

The other side of the equation offers no more hope of accurate resolution. T in the Fisher scheme represented the total number

[1] *Econ. Hist. Rev.* (1962–3), p. 280.

of transactions, or the total amount of trade undertaken in a given time period, and the difficulties are not eased by stretching the time period to a century or more. Historians have tried to assess movements in T by reasoning as to probable movements in the physical output of certain goods. Services have generally been entirely ignored. There is, moreover, practically no important class of commodities whose output can be assessed with any pretence at accuracy in the sixteenth and seventeenth centuries. Agriculture, for example, is full of unknowns; we might hazard that total agricultural output – in physical terms – lagged somewhat behind an advancing population, but this would mean more if we were less ignorant about the precise dimensions of the population increase. Trends in the production of woollen cloth are equally uncertain; total output in the mid-seventeenth century was probably greater than in the early sixteenth, but to what extent it is impossible to say. Trends in other important industries, like building, the production of leather, boots and shoes, and food and drink offer even less hope of accurate quantification. Quite often, historians have leaned back on the vaguest of generalities, like citing Professor Nef's 'industrial revolution' to signify increasing output, sometimes without the very necessary qualification that the increases he found were in the minor, less important industries of Tudor and Stuart England. Their importance from the viewpoint of total output was far outweighed by those industries previously mentioned.

When we come to P the problems are reduced but not entirely eliminated. P, in the Fisher equation, represented the average prices of all goods and services sold for money in a given time period. The first difficulty is that we do not have information about *all* prices, and the gaps include many of the most important items of expenditure. Practically nothing is known, for example, about the price of bread; not enough is known about the price of beer; we are ignorant about house rent; and our knowledge of payments for services is practically non-existent.[1] Secondly, many of those prices that we do have are probably not representative of the prices paid by individual consumers; some, especially the sale

[1] A. P. Usher criticised existing indexes in 1931 for failing to give due importance to three classes of items: wages, transport services and finished manufactures. Also they frequently ignored the geographical element ('Prices of Wheat and Commodity Price Indexes for England', *The Review of Economic Statistics*, XIII (1931), 103–13).

prices drawn from great estates, are more representative of whole-sale prices than retail ones; others, especially those purchase prices drawn from institutions like schools, colleges and hospitals display occasionally some of the characteristics of contracted bargains – relatively fixed prices, with fluctuations absorbed by changes in quality rather than in price. Thirdly, historians have cheerfully constructed price indexes, or have borrowed the con-structions of others, and have used these to represent P, thinking thereby they are representing the 'general level of prices', with-out knowing or acknowledging either that this is an abstraction almost unrealisable in practice, or that existing indexes are often constructed for specific purposes, purposes which bear little relation to the Fisher ideal.

Bearing some of these qualifications in mind readers might well begin to question the usefulness of some recent writing on the price rise. Mr. Brenner, for example, asks us to look seriously at tables and graphs depicting increases in the total additions to the stock of Spanish treasure (not European, nor English, either of which might be more relevant) and to seek correlations with movements in the price indexes constructed originally by Phelps Brown and Hopkins to measure, in a fashion admitted rightly by the authors to be very approximate, changes in the purchasing power of the money wages of building operatives at Oxford. Seeking correlations between this particular M and that particular P is to indulge in crudities never resorted to by Professor Hamilton, who appears to be the object of Mr. Brenner's demolition exercise, and the reasoning must disturb not only the purists.

Apart from these difficulties of application – what we might call the divorce between ideal and reality in applying the Fisher equation – we have also to deal with the problems posed by recalcitrant 'facts'. The English price rise, as we have seen, was for long explained solely in terms of the operation of two monetary factors: debasement and enhancement of the coinage, operating in the first half of the sixteenth century,[1] and the influx of Spanish bullion getting underway from the 1540s onwards. Both

[1] The clearest accounts of the great debasement are those in the works of Oman and Feavearyear cited above. They should be read in conjunction with the recent careful corrective of C. E. Challis, 'The De-basement of the Coinage, 1542–1551', *Econ. Hist. Rev.*, 2nd series, XX, no. 3 (1967), 441–66.

these explanations have met a barrage of criticism. It has been pointed out, for example, that debasement is an insufficient explanation of the price rise, even in the first half of the century, because the price rise was underway before the great debasement following 1542 really began. Nor can this preceding rise be explained as a result of the relatively minor reduction of 1526, because, secondly, there is no very exact synchronisation between debasement generally and the rise in prices. Thirdly, historians have puzzled over the fact that prices rose very unevenly, when, it was argued, a mere change in monetary standards might be expected to increase prices uniformly. Fourthly, prices generally did not rise to the same extent as the intrinsic value of the coin fell. Finally the price rise continued long after debasement came to an end with Elizabeth's near restoration of pre-1526 standards in 1560–1.[1]

Greater objections have been levelled against the view that the rise in prices was sustained during and after the great debasement, if not before, by the influx of treasure, especially silver, from the New World. Professor Hamilton's brief indications as to how this might have been achieved have already been mentioned.[2] Difficulties have arisen through looking at the process from an English rather than a Spanish viewpoint, looking at the forces making for an influx into England rather than those working for the efflux from Spain. It has been argued that the most important avenue of entry must have been to settle trade balances, and it has appeared to some, though perhaps erroneously, that work on English commerce has suggested that the trade balance was frequently, perhaps chronically, negative rather than positive. Little specie, it has been argued, could have entered by these means.[3] Economic historians have been able to make little either of the second avenue of entry, through diverging bimetallic ratios. One difficulty is that increased imports of one metal were presumably balanced in value terms by increased exports of the other, leaving no change in the total value of precious metals in circulation. As for smuggling gold and silver, if it was carried on, and if it was successful, then it obviously escaped record. On the

[1] Much of this criticism is retailed in Brenner, *Econ. Hist. Rev.*, 1961–2.

[2] See above, p. 28, note 1.

[3] But see also pp. 51–2 where it is suggested that such conclusions are ill-supported and certainly premature.

whole, however, absence of record has been taken to imply absence of deed. Hamilton himself argued that shipments avoiding Spain were inconsiderable and that losses via privateering were negligible.[1] The net result of these enquiries is to doubt whether considerable quantities of Spanish silver reached England before 1630, and to argue that much of the considerable quantity which then arrived and was coined through agreements between Charles I and Spain was subsequently exported.[2] All these arguments have done much to devalue the Hamilton approach, and by implication the historical validity of the quantity theory. Nevertheless, it is still being argued that the quantity of precious metal used as coin in England increased. If it did not come from Spain, it must have come from internal sources.[3] To this, and related points, we shall return later.

Hamilton's work, and general quantity theory notions, have received also a certain amount of criticism from continental scholars. François Simiand's grand survey of European price history[4] drew attention to Hamilton's use of figures for *imports*, rather than the total *stock* of precious metals, and to his failure to explore the reasons why prices appear to rise less than increases in the total stock. Much greater attention ought to be paid to money, he suggested, and to its velocity, rather than just to precious metals. He criticised Hamilton for his blindness to all but his own particular thesis, for not investigating thoroughly the extent to which prices were affected by factors other than M. This involved paying much more attention to the behaviour of T and V in the Fisher equation. Nevertheless, Simiand was favourably inclined towards the Hamilton thesis, and his own work is a thoughtful exercise in the application of the Fisher equation to explain European price behaviour generally. The American scholar J. U. Nef, although severely critical of Hamilton's 'profit-inflation' thesis, was favourably inclined to the view that the rise in prices was the result of a decline in the exchange value of precious metals, consequent upon the discovery of new sources

[1] Hamilton, *American Treasure and the Price Revolution in Spain, 1501–1650*, chapter II, *passim*.

[2] This is the conclusion reached by Brenner, *Econ. Hist. Rev.*, 1962–3, from which most of this discussion is drawn.

[3] This is the line taken by Brenner, *ibid.*, p. 278.

[4] *Recherches anciennes et nouvelles sur le mouvement général des prix du XVIe au XIXe siècle* (Paris, 1932).

of supply, and he helped to remedy one weakness in earlier explanations by pointing to the possibility of a considerable increase in European silver output before New World treasure began to arrive in Spain.[1] More recent work has tended to question the validity of both the Hamilton and Fisher approaches. Professor Cipolla, in particular, opened up a lively debate when he argued in 1955 that the movement of Italian prices after 1550 reveals no correlation with what is known about imports of treasure into Italy, and pleaded for an alternative approach to the study of inflation, employing more modern tools of analysis and concentrating on the behaviour of population and investment.[2] Some price historians had indeed already stressed the importance of demographic factors in explaining the behaviour of prices.[3] Dr. Hammarström herself surveyed these criticisms, took the Fisher equation to task, and contributed some preliminary findings on Swedish prices in the period 1460–1560 which cast doubt on the traditional explanation. She argued that current prices, especially those of food, were rising from about 1490 onwards, well before much treasure reached Europe, and that manufacturing prices rose later and rather less. If these prices are converted to silver-content prices, however, then owing to a series of debasements, the price rise vanishes, except in the cases of certain foodstuffs. From this she concludes, 'There is no doubt that silver kept its value, and even rose in value, compared with most other commodities.'[4] Finally she too pleaded for a more modern approach to the analysis of price changes.

[1] J. U. Nef, 'Silver Production in Central Europe, 1450–1618', *Journal of Political Economy*, XLIX (1941), 575–91.

[2] C. M. Cipolla, 'La Prétendue "Revolution des Prix": Réflexions sur l'experiénce italienne', *Annales: Economies, Sociétés, Civilisations*, X (1955), 513–16.

[3] Especially M. J. Elsas (*Umriss einer Geschichte der Preise und Löhne in Deutschland vom ausgehenden Mittelalter bis zum Beginn des Neunzehnten Jahrhunderts*, Leiden, 1936–49), who early revealed to English audiences some of his important findings in 'Price Data from Munich, 1500–1700', *Economic History*, III (1935), 63–78.

[4] Hammarström, *op. cit.*, p. 146. This is later slightly qualified: 'The inference to be drawn from these considerations is that it is doubtful whether any conceivable properly weighted general index would exhibit a continuous rise in the price of silver in terms of commodities during the period 1460–1560. It might well only establish that the value of silver was more or less unchanged.' (*idem*).

Irving Fisher's version of the quantity theory has long been subjected to criticism, both by those economists who found the equation useful and those who did not. Many theorists working within the theory objected to the notion that changes in M had little or no effect on V or T and therefore induced proportionate changes in P. They argued that changes in the money stock could lead to changes in V and T, and especially popular has been the notion that decreases in M (the supply of money) could lead to increases in its velocity. In other words, given a scarcity of the monetary stock men will find ways of using that stock more efficiently. Thus a decline in M need not necessarily lead to a decline in P. The logical corollary of this is that an increase in M need not necessarily lead to an increase in P. Even if T remained unchanged, which was unlikely, V may decline. Given an abundant M men may have no need to economise in the use of the money stock. Others stressed the importance of autonomous or independent changes in V or T, arguing that these may be sufficient to account for almost all the changes experienced in P.[1]

Some economists found the equation unhelpful. Chief amongst these was J. M. Keynes, who expressed dissatisfaction with the prevailing generalised approach to price analysis, and abandoned the quantity theory because it dealt in variables which were inappropriate or irrelevant to the problems he was pursuing. His scrutiny of the factors governing the short-run behaviour of prices, output and employment led to decreasing attention being paid to purely monetary elements and much more attention being paid to variables and concepts which do not figure in the Fisher equation, such as the propensities governing the level of savings and investment, and the relationships between these two variables. His criticism of the short-term usefulness of the Fisher equation has been transferred by implication to question its long-run validity.

[1] This and the following section owes a great deal to the editorial comment, and selections from authorities, in E. Dean (ed.), *The Controversy over the Quantity Theory of Money* (Boston, 1965).

Real or Physical Explanations

'REAL' explanations, which placed less emphasis on changes in the monetary sphere than they did on other, physical factors operating on prices, have never been entirely absent from discussions of secular changes in the price level. They were present, as has been shown, in contemporary discussion of inflation in Tudor England, but later such explanations became more characteristic of discussions about inflation in periods other than the sixteenth and seventeenth centuries. Even when the quantity theory was most fashionable there were heretics who were prepared to argue that changes in price levels were only remotely linked, if at all, with changes in the availability of monetary supplies. Irving Fisher felt it necessary, for example, to castigate David A. Wells, author of *Recent Economic Changes* (1890), who had argued that the long deflation of the later nineteenth century could be explained almost entirely by shifts in the supply and demand schedules of important commodities, and by falling costs, the most important of which was the dramatic drop in freight rates.[1] To the quantity theorists this was anathema, for they explained it almost entirely in terms of an increasing demand for precious metals, which was a function of increasing monetary requirements, running ahead of the supply of precious metals. This situation, it was argued, was not corrected until the discoveries of gold in South Africa and the Yukon at the end of the century shifted the balance in the other direction. The debate has continued and more recently the quantity theory viewpoint has been strongly challenged and new physical explanations are thrust to the forefront.[2]

As far as the inflation of the sixteenth century was concerned the implications of these debates were ignored. Down to the

[1] I. Fisher, *op. cit.*, pp. 174–81.

[2] See W. W. Rostow, *The British Economy of the Nineteenth Century* (Oxford, 1948), pp. 145–60, for a résumé of the debate; and E. H. Phelps Brown and S. A. Ozga, 'Economic Growth and the Price Level', *Economic Journal*, LXV (1955), 1–18, for a challenging physical interpretation of nineteenth-century price fluctuations.

1950s, it was accounted for, with exceptions only amongst continental scholars, almost entirely in the old monetary terms. By the 1950s, however, the path was open to interpretations of a different kind, and it was prepared in a number of different ways. One was the work here and abroad of major price historians, especially those influenced by the International Scientific Committee. Their principal contribution was the amassing and processing of new price materials, which revealed the inadequacies of the data provided by Rogers, D'Avenel and others, data which had been used extensively by commentators from Wiebe onwards. Their contribution thus undermined faith in old beliefs and furnished the raw materials for new interpretations. Also, economic historians usually take a decade or more to comprehend the changes wrought by their more theoretical colleagues, and by the 1950s it was clear that many historians had absorbed the implications of the various attacks on the quantity theory and the Fisher equation. New methods of analysing price changes were in fashion. These were essentially disaggregative rather than aggregative. Economists were more inclined to explain changes in a price index by reference to the various real factors influencing its constituent items than by general monetary forces operating on the whole index. A third path was prepared by economic historians operating in periods other than the sixteenth and seventeenth centuries, who were providing explanations of changing price levels cast almost entirely in real terms. Apart from new interpretations of nineteenth-century price trends, mention should also be made of the outstanding work on the later Middle Ages of Professor M. M. Postan, who continually drew attention to the important effects that population changes had upon prices and wages. His work provided an explanation of wage and price movements that virtually ignored monetary factors, but its implications for later centuries were not immediately seized upon.[1] Finally, we must draw attention to historians operating in fields other than price history, but who nevertheless produced results which caused students of the Tudor inflation to question, and in some cases to reject, many of the assumptions on which old arguments were based. The work on sixteenth and

[1] Especially important was his 'Some Economic Evidence of Declining Population in the Later Middle Ages', *Economic History Review*, 2nd series, II (1950), 221–46, but strong hints had been dropped in his 'The Fifteenth Century', *ibid.*, IX (1939), 160–7.

seventeenth century English trade of F. J. Fisher and L. Stone supplies perhaps an outstanding example.[1] Signs that all these things were getting through can be detected in Dr. Kerridge's grumble in 1953, 'We are not yet justified in ascribing the inflation of the sixteenth and seventeenth centuries merely and at bottom to debasement of the coinage and the influx of precious metals, since such theories have not yet been proved historically.'[2] This came in the course of his own important paper on rising rents, a paper which seemed to argue that rising rent was an (if not the) important inflationary force in the sixteenth and seventeenth centuries.

On the whole, however, the reaction appeared first amongst continental scholars. Professor Cipolla sparked off a lively debate in *Annales* with his sceptical short article of 1955 on Italian prices. In the same issue there appeared a long article on Belgian prices, challenging a number of widely held beliefs, especially the view that wages tended to lag seriously behind prices in the Low Countries, and suggesting that debasement and the increase in the quantity of money were as much consequences of increasing demands for money as independent causes of the price rise.[3] Miss Hammarström also suggested that debasement might well have been induced by inflationary pressures within the economy.[4]

At the same time there also appeared an important article by two English economists, Professor Phelps Brown and Miss S. V. Hopkins, arguing that the upward but divergent paths of agricultural, industrial and labour prices in England, France and parts of Germany in the sixteenth and early seventeenth centuries, revealed evidence of considerable population pressure.[5] The same analysis and conclusion was later extended by them to other areas

[1] F. J. Fisher, 'Commercial Trends and Policy in Sixteenth Century England', *Economic History Review*, X (1940), 95–117; 'London's Export Trade in the Early Seventeenth Century', *ibid.*, 2nd series, III (1950), 151–61; L. Stone, 'Elizabethan Overseas Trade', *ibid.*, 2nd series, II (1949–50), 30–58.

[2] E. Kerridge, 'The Movement of Rent, 1540–1640,' *ibid.*, 2nd series, VI (1953), 16–34.

[3] C. Verlinden, J. Craeybeckx, E. Scholliers, 'Mouvements des prix et des salaires en Belgique en XVIe siècle, *Annales: Économies, Sociétés, Civilisations*, 10 (1955), 173–98.

[4] Hammarström, *op. cit.*, pp. 130–1, 152–4. See also p. 35 above.

[5] 'Wage-rates and Prices: Evidence for Population Pressure in the Sixteenth Century', *Economica*, XXIV (1957), 289–306.

in Germany, to Austria and even to Spain.[1] It was on these foundations that Y. S. Brenner built his re-examination of the causes of the English price rise, a not wholly successful attempt to marry new and old interpretations, with the newer, real or physical explanations given perhaps pride of place.

The analysis of the 'real' school is essentially disaggregative. It deals less with general movements of whole price indexes than with the relative movements of their constituent parts. It has long been noticed by price historians, certainly from Rogers onwards, that agricultural prices, for example, rose very much more than industrial ones in this period. Similarly Rogers and others have noted that money wages lagged behind general price indexes, combining both agricultural and industrial products.[2] Professor Hamilton, in fact, argued from this last feature that 'capitalism' was stimulated in this period by the lag of wages, an important part of total costs, behind prices, producing a situation of profit inflation.[3] J. U. Nef, however, severely criticised the 'profit inflation' thesis, a demolition exercise completed in 1956 by David Felix.[4] A product of these criticisms was the renewed realisation that money wages lagged behind agricultural prices to a very much greater extent than industrial ones. Indeed they may not have lagged behind industrial prices at all. As far as

[1] 'Builders' Wage-rates, Prices and Population: Some Further Evidence', *ibid.*, XXVI (1959), 18–38.

[2] See Rogers, *op. cit.*, IV, 725, where he comments, 'It will be clear from these facts that the producer of animal food, grain and other agricultural necessities commanded a better market than the dealer in any other article of value did, and that . . . labour and those commodities the value of which was principally derived from labour, partook in the least degree of that rise which was effected in all commodities, glass alone excepted.' Rogers could never completely make up his mind about population growth, but on the whole did not think it began until after *c.* 1580. (V, 782, 788).

[3] The idea is first introduced in his 'American Treasure and the Rise of Capitalism (1500–1700)', *op. cit.*, pp. 349–57. Keynes was so taken with the idea that it led him to say of the years 1575 to 1620 that it was a period 'when any level-headed person in England disposed to make money could hardly help doing so'. Keynes, *op. cit.*, II, 154.

[4] J. U. Nef, 'Prices and Industrial Capitalism in France and England, 1540–1640', *Economic History Review*, VII (1937), 155–85; D. Felix, 'Profit Inflation and Industrial Growth: The Historic Record', *Quarterly Journal of Economics*, LXX (1956), 441–63.

industrial 'capitalists' were concerned, therefore, there may not have been any profit inflation. It was left, however, to Phelps Brown and Hopkins to suggest that these divergent movements indicated population pressure, and that a growing population was an important, if not the most important, general cause of the sixteenth- and seventeenth-century inflation.

The case rests on the basic premise that agriculture was unable to expand its total output to meet all the requirements of an expanding population – not only for food but also for industrial raw materials, construction materials and fuel. This gave rise, from the early sixteenth century, to fluctuating but sustained increases in agricultural product prices, and, under the twin impetus of rising prices plus increased competition for holdings, to rising rents. At the same time the increasing population produced a buoyant labour market, and competition for jobs kept wages from rising to the same extent as agricultural prices. Nevertheless wages did rise, and this, coupled with increases in raw material costs, reacted on industrial product prices. Industrial prices rose less than agricultural ones, however, because demand and supply elasticities were greater, because industry was able to increase its productivity rather more than agriculture and because rent was not such an important cost element. It has also been suggested that the rate of increase in the demand for industrial products in general was less than that for agricultural products, owing to the decline in the real incomes of many wage earners and the shift of income in favour of those – the yeomen in particular – with a high propensity to save.[1]

Probably the clearest statement of the 'real' explanation has come not from a historian but from an economist, Geoffrey Maynard, in his *Economic Development and the Price Level* (1962). Maynard rejects as utterly inadequate the quantity theory explanations of secular price changes, citing recent work on the nineteenth century as historical support. His own thesis is that inflation and deflation have proceeded historically almost entirely from dissimilar rates of agricultural and industrial advance, producing upward and downward shifts in agricultural prices which have had important cost and demand repercussions in the economy as a whole. As far as the sixteenth century is concerned, the analysis draws heavily on Nef and Felix to propose a thesis very similar to that suggested in the previous paragraph,

[1] See, for example, Dr. Bowden in *AHEW*, *op. cit.*, pp. 607–9.

which in turn draws heavily on Phelps Brown and Brenner.

The arguments of the 'real' school can be criticised on a number of grounds. First of all we know precious little about the population of the sixteenth century.[1] It is clear that between the mid-fifteenth century and the end of the seventeenth century England's population grew considerably, and it is probable that much of this growth was concentrated in the period from about 1480 to about 1630.[2] But we are not yet sure precisely when population began to expand, when it eventually contracted, whether growth proceeded evenly through time, whether it was uniformly spread over England, how fast it took place, and so on.[3] One cannot help feeling that the Spanish bullion thesis was seized so avidly because of its numerous advantages: first of all, given the lack of historical evidence it could not be disproved; secondly, it was so disarmingly simple and obvious that it was unnecessary to prove it; and lastly (invisible) fluctuations in its flow could be offered as explanations of many price movements for which no other apparent cause was readily available. We must avoid, however, making population pressure do all the work which was formerly undertaken by Spanish treasure.[4]

[1] The best summary of our ignorance, and of the problems of the period generally, is F. J. Fisher's masterly inaugural lecture, 'The Sixteenth and Seventeenth Centuries: The Dark Ages in English Economic History?', *Economica*, XXIV (1957), 1–18.

[2] Though it has to be pointed out that much of the evidence for this has come from the scrutiny of relative price movements. Thus there is an enormous danger of explaining price movements by referring to population and accounting for the latter by referring to prices.

[3] There are hopes, however, that some of these questions may eventually be answered through the efforts of the Cambridge Group for the History of Population and Social Structure, founded in 1964. The most interesting of its contributions to date is E. A. Wrigley's 'Family Limitation in Pre-Industrial England', *Economic History Review*, 2nd series, XIX (1966), 82–109.

[4] Brenner, for example, invokes a slackening of population growth in the mid-sixteenth century to explain the pause in inflation felt in those years. He suggests, 'Food prices had risen to an extent that incomes no longer permitted early marriages and the survival of large families.' No evidence whatsoever is offered, however, in support of these demographic notions. Professor Fisher has recently argued that he is probably correct in suggesting that there was a demographic pause but that its causes were, 'more likely to be found in an epidemic to which the Tudor Englishman could offer less effective resistance

One problem is how to explain the stepped profile revealed in Fig. 1, and especially the marked rises of the second decade of the sixteenth century, the years 1544–51, the mid-'70s, the '90s, and the late 1620s and early '30s, periods which precede the eventual establishment of new price plateaux. Although a demographic explanation is not inconceivable, other real (and monetary) elements ought to be taken into consideration. The two periods of steepest inflation, those of the mid-'40s and the 1590s, coincided with years of war and enormous increases in government expenditure, furnished by methods – heavy taxation, borrowing and land sales – which were likely to have increased total spending, especially on provisions, at the expense of private saving. The mid-1590s witnessed also four terrible harvests in a row, while the 1630s saw only one good harvest in ten years.[1] The less marked rise of the mid-'70s has been tentatively ascribed to rising export demands for English grain.[2] Short-run factors such as these could clearly rack prices and costs to new levels, from which an underlying growth of population would make it difficult for them to descend.

Some room should also be found for monetary factors. Maynard comments in one place, 'It will be noted that no reference has been made to the quantity of money. The reason for this is the belief that, in the long run, the quantity of money is more likely to adjust to prices and to the "needs of trade" than the other way round. In the short run, an inelastic supply of money may play a part in bringing booms to an end, although the community is usually able to economise in the use of its money, so that even an absolutely constant stock of money can support varying levels of income and prices.'[3] It is clear that such opinions owe much to the developments in economic theory to which attention has been drawn, and they owe much also to the fact that in modern societies the money supply is almost completely elastic: the

---

than he could to an epidemic of chastity,' namely the great influenza epidemic which raged from 1556. See Brenner, *Econ. Hist. Rev.*, 1962–3, p. 284; Fisher, *Econ. Hist. Rev.* 1965, p. 125.

[1] W. G. Hoskins, 'Harvest Fluctuations and English Economic History, 1480–1619', *Agricultural History Review*, 12 (1964), 28–46, and 'Harvest Fluctuations and English Economic History, 1620–1759', *ibid.*, 16 (1968), 15–31.

[2] F. J. Fisher, 'Influenza and Inflation', p. 124.

[3] Maynard, *op. cit.*, p. 69, note 1.

authorities are able to expand and contract the money supply according to the dictates of the economy. But in economies like those of the sixteenth century, where coins were the most important forms of money, where continual debasements might be frowned upon, and where non-metallic forms of currency made little progress, the currency supply can hardly be described as completely elastic. In these circumstances the stock of precious metals inevitably played a more important part than it has done in recent times.

There is also a tendency, moreover, for some economic historians to over-estimate the extent to which debasement of the coinage in the sixteenth century was simply a response to growing demands for currency within the economy and to under-estimate the part played by the voracious appetites of impoverished royal finances. Certainly none of the arguments commonly used to deny a connection between debasement in general and inflation have much force when applied to the great debasement of Henry VIII and Edward VI. These arguments are that there was no very exact synchronisation between the course of debasement and the movement of prices; that the rise in current prices in the great debasement period was less than the degree of debasement involved;[1] and thirdly that there was no uniformity of price increase.[2] The first point can be countered readily. Our knowledge about the course of debasement has until recently been extremely deficient. It is often taken for granted that changes became effective from the day that they were promulgated. Too little attention has been paid to the delays and difficulties inherent in the administering of such changes, and to the timing of issues from the Mint. Although in the great debasement the first changes in standards were evident in 1542, it was not until 1544–5 that large issues of debased coins began to tumble from the Mint.[3] Secondly, purely monetary factors were not the only regulators of prices: the harvests above all tended to produce distortions which were entirely unrelated to the course of debasement. The vagaries of nature produced enormous fluctuations in the prices of agricultural commodities, which loom very

[1] So that an index calculated on the basis of silver-content would show an overall fall. This was noted by Wiebe, Simiand and Usher amongst others.

[2] See Brenner, *Econ. Hist. Rev.* (1961–2), pp. 227–30.

[3] The recent work of Challis (*op. cit.*) has confirmed these views.

large in both the economy and our price indexes, and it is therefore not surprising that no very exact synchronisation can be found.

The second argument, that prices generally rose less than the degree of debasement, is also of doubtful validity. It comes from the construction of silver-content price indexes, which tend to show a fall in the great debasement period. Such indexes are usually constructed by reference to the dates on which changes in monetary standards were first ordered to be made. We have already pointed to the delays in the system, which would cause such an index to misrepresent actuality until the Mint began to issue debased coins. More important is the fact that debased coin did not immediately, or completely, supercede other coins in circulation. Non-debased coins might circulate,[1] as also would foreign coins. The total monetary stock did not, therefore, increase in proportion to the 'official' decline in intrinsic values. It would tend to increase less. In other words, the construction of silver-content prices by these means tends to over-correct the price rise; it is too severe a deflator of current prices.[2]

The third argument, that prices rose at often very dissimilar rates, displays a similar lack of sophistication. Prices would rise at similar rates only if demand was a constant function of money, so that an increase in the quantity of money led to an equivalent increase in demand; it would happen only if this increase in demand was expended in a manner exactly proportionate to that ruling before such an increase; and it would happen only if supply elasticities were similar throughout the system. The

[1] Though there would be a tendency for those containing most precious metal gradually to disappear from circulation.

[2] This has been noticed by J. D. Gould, *Econ. Hist. Rev.* (1964), 256–9. Silver-prices were first used to try to establish whether in fact there were changes in the respective exchange values of precious metals and commodities, and to facilitate international comparisons. Their inadequacies have frequently been noted, particularly by Simiand (*op. cit.*, pp. 41–2), Elsas (*Econ. Hist.*, 1935, pp. 63–4), and Beveridge (*op. cit.*, pp. xlvii–xlix). Apart from those problems already noted, and the problems of which metal to use as the basis for conversion, the chief difficulty is that money had a value beyond that of the precious metal contained within it. Seignorage and Mint charges alone would ensure this. The public certainly did not always reckon a coin exactly according to its intrinsic worth, although they might be sensitive to abrupt and flagrant changes in standards.

unlikelihood of any of these provisos makes this objection hardly worth considering.

We shall not begin to further our understanding unless we make a serious effort to understand exactly how debasement, etc., affected prices, and this means abandoning rather *simpliste* quantity theory notions. A severe debasement, such as that suffered from the 1540s onwards, affected prices and purchasing power in a number of ways. First of all it immediately altered the exchange rate and resulted in rising demands for exports and some rise in import prices. It would not be surprising to find that both these forces had inflationary effects, and that their subsequent influence on English prices would vary enormously. Secondly, debasement increased the incomes of those who took money or metal to the Mint, and, above all, it increased the incomes of those, especially the Crown, who took a cut out of the proceeds of minting. We must not forget the enormous fiscal pressures which caused Henry VIII and his immediate successors to milk the coinage. Much more attention could be paid to the great increases in royal purchasing power which resulted, and its inflationary effects via heavy outlays on provisions for war, etc. Some price increases would result in these 'real' ways, through changes in the supply and demand for goods and services, but some also appear to have resulted from simple adjustments to prices so as to compensate for the reduced intrinsic value of the coinage. That this went on is suggested by the proclamations which usually accompanied enhancement or debasement and which invariably forbade the raising of prices.[1] Enhancements were more likely to result in such compensatory upward price adjustments than debasement, since the alterations were more open, and necessarily more widely publicised. A corollary of this, of course, is that in the worst period of debasement there may well have been something of a flight from money – an increase in propensities to consume – among people eager to get rid of base coin. Neither enhancement nor debasement, however, was likely to result in all prices being affected, if only because of ignorance, delays in the spread of awareness of such changes, and the possible deterrent effect of attempts to control such price adjustments. That all prices should have risen, or have risen equally, are the last things we should expect.

Even apart from debasement, however, the 'real' case, and

[1] See, for example, Oman, *op. cit.*, p. 252.

especially the heavy concentration upon population growth, is incomplete in another sense. No one has yet suggested, for example, that the population advance of the sixteenth century was more rapid than that of the thirteenth or of the eighteenth, yet the rise in prices in the Tudor period was far greater than that experienced in either of the other periods. If nothing else we have to explain why prices – and silver-content prices in particular – were able to expand so markedly. The sixteenth-century price rise has been called the greatest specie-based inflation of which we have record. It is unlikely that this could have occurred without an increase in the monetary stock, and it is improbable that the latter had no connection with the inflow into Europe of Spanish-American silver.[1]

Conclusion

THE argument about the causes of inflation is largely about whether money should be assigned an active or a passive role. On the whole the monetary school have argued that its role was an active one, that monetary changes *caused* the price rise.[2] The real school, however, have relegated monetary factors to a passive

[1] Some countries and some indexes show a rise in silver-content prices before much Spanish-American silver began to arrive. See, for example, F. P. Braudel and F. Spooner, 'Prices in Europe from 1450 to 1750', in E. E. Rich and C. E. Wilson (eds.), *The Cambridge Economic History of Europe* (Cambridge, 1967), IV, 394, 400–2, 470–1. There are two possible explanations of this early rise. One is that it is connected with increases in the European stock of silver stemming from the increases in European silver mining to which Professor Nef drew attention (see above p. 35, note 1) Another (and more likely) reason for the changed relationship between silver and goods is that it reflects an increasing scarcity of agricultural products in relation to the demands for them rather than an increasing abundance of silver. It must always be remembered that most indexes are dominated by agricultural product prices, especially wheat prices. Hence the significance of Miss Hammarström's remarks cited above, p. 35.

[2] The obverse of this is, of course, that prices are assigned a purely passive role. See I. Fisher's statement, '*The price level is normally the one absolutely passive element in the equation of exchange*. It is controlled solely by the other elements and the causes antecedent to them,

role, arguing that the inflation was caused principally by divergences in the population-resource balance which inflated agricultural prices, wages and costs. The view adopted here is that over the period as a whole 'real' factors, and especially the growing imbalance between the growth of population and agricultural output, offer the more satisfactory general explanation of inflation,[1] but that its pace may have been exacerbated in England in the 1540s and early '50s by the great debasement. Even if the emphasis is placed in this way, it must still be acknowledged that increases in the money supply and/or increasing efficiency of its use, were necessary concomitants of the whole process.[2] In other words, using Fisher's shorthand, that increases in MV were necessary concomitants of increases in PT. Despite all the objections previously raised, no one can seriously deny that a considerable increase in PT took place. The total output of the economy in 1640 can hardly have been less than it was in 1500, and was probably considerably greater. Agriculture must have expanded its total output as additional factors of production were drawn into use, and the number of industries of any significance which declined were more than offset by those which expanded. At the same time, there are practically no commodities, amongst those of which we have price records, whose prices actually diminished over the whole period 1500–1640. Thorold Rogers found one – glass; wax has been mentioned as another possibility. Even though this list is probably incomplete, it is difficult to believe that there are important omissions. The national product

---

but exerts no control over them.' (I. Fisher, *op. cit.*, p. 182, his italics); and 'The price level is the effect and cannot be the cause of change in the other factors,' (*ibid.*, p. 182).

[1] One test of any explanation of the price revolution must be whether it has any general application. Inflation was a European experience, and New World treasure was once seen as a plausible general European cause. Population pressure meets this test, and provides a more satisfactory answer to many questions that the bullionists had left unanswered. The best discussion of Europe's population in this period is K. F. Helleiner, 'The Population of Europe from the Black Death to the Eve of the Vital Revolution', in Rich and Wilson, *op. cit.*, 1–95.

[2] The problem of money supply was solved by each country in its own individual way, though there are obvious similarities in the solutions to this common problem.

expressed in terms of current prices must have grown. It is this which is represented by PT in the Fisher equation and its growth must have been counterbalanced by an equivalent increase in MV. Note that we are not arguing that the increase in PT was *caused* by increases in MV; its increase was caused essentially by factors operating outside this equation.[1]

One thing we have to explain, therefore, is how this increase in MV came about. What weight to attach to M and what to V is virtually impossible to decide. All that we can say is that V increased;[2] all the weight cannot be attached to V, however, since there is evidence also of an increase in M, even apart from the limited increases derived from negotiable paper, copper tokens, etc. In this respect the issues of the Mint are extremely interesting. The figures of issues show a strong generally rising trend in value terms from about 1540 to 1640, following upon two centuries in which the trend of Mint issues was relatively stable.[3] Although these issues do not in themselves constitute evidence of an increase in the total value in circulation, they are strongly suggestive of such an increase. What caused the Mint to increase so greatly its value of output? Part of the increase, especially during the years 1542–51, was certainly the direct result of debasement, which worked to increase the value of Mint issues in two ways. One was by coining more from a given weight of precious metal, the other was by attracting new supplies of metal (or old coins) to the Mint. Over the whole period 1540–1640, however, the overall degree of debasement was relatively light,[4] and this is especially true of the years following 1551.[5] The high level of the Mint's silver issues in the century after 1550 cannot be ascribed to the higher nominal returns exacted from alterations of the Mint-price via debasement. The other great

[1] Except, possibly, during the great debasement.

[2] Along the lines suggested above, p. 29.

[3] After a pause in the mid-seventeenth century this rise is resumed in the last decades. Figures of Mint issues are to be found in Sir John Craig, *The Mint* (Cambridge, 1953), Appendix I.

[4] The quantity of silver in £1, for example, shrank from 2,560 Troy grains in 1540 to 1,858 in 1640. This is a much smaller diminution than that which occurred from, say, 1340 (5,332 grains) to 1540 (2,560). See Craig, *op. cit.*, p. 74.

[5] In 1552 1,920 grains of silver were contained in £1, in 1601, 1,858. Thereafter there was no change until 1816.

49

regulator of Mint output was the outcome of a calculus involving the overall availability of the precious metals and the monetary requirements of society. The latter was certainly increasing; but what of the former? Two points are worth making here. First of all, it is interesting to recall that the fifteenth century was marked by long and persistent complaints of shortages of money.[1] The complaints may have been precipitated by numerous short-term events, balance of payments difficulties for instance, but they may also have reflected basic shortages of precious metals, especially silver. These shortages, especially that of silver, have been seen as one very important, underlying reason for the continuous debasements of the later Middle Ages.[2] It is arguable that these scarcities continued into the early sixteenth century, precipitating further rounds of English and indeed European debasements.[3] Certainly this is offered as an excuse by the English authorities for enhancement and debasement in 1526 and 1542–4,[4] though strong fiscal pressures were also present and resulted, in the later period, in over-indulgence in the exercise. Thereafter the complaints of scarcity slacken, and despite the near restoration of pre-1526 standards in the recoinage of 1560–1, no further serious debasements of silver took place until relatively modern times. If debasement was precipitated by scarcity then that condition seems to have been eased in England by the mid-sixteenth century. Secondly, for a century and a half after the first permanent issue of gold coins in the mid-fourteenth century, issues of gold coins far exceeded in value those of silver. There may be evidence here of the silver famine to which contemporaries repeatedly drew attention.[5] Then, from about 1520 onwards Mint issues of silver

[1] These are retailed in H. A. Miskimin, 'Monetary Movements and Market Structure – Forces for Contraction in Fourteenth and Fifteenth Century England', *Journal of Economic History*, XXIV (1964), 470–490; see also R. D. Ware's discussion of this paper (pp. 491–5).

[2] The best recent discussion is C. M. Cipolla, 'Currency Depreciation in Medieval Europe', *Economic History Review*, 2nd series, XV (1963), 413–22.

[3] Miss Hamarström seems to be suggesting this (*op. cit.*, pp. 153–4). Debasement in one country would tend to put pressures on others to follow suit, rather like devaluation in the 1930s.

[4] Tawney and Power, *op. cit.*, II, 176–7; *Letters and Papers, Henry VIII*, XIX, pt. 1, pp. xxxv–vi; Feavearyear, *op. cit.*, pp. 50–3.

[5] A fascinating discussion of this silver famine, which was European in its incidence, is to be found in the important article by A. M.

began to exceed, and from the 1540s onwards enormously to exceed, those of gold, which remained until the early seventeenth century on a par with their 1350–1520 levels. From the early eighteenth century onwards silver issues again became negligible. Looked at over this long period of time, 1350–1800, we do have to explain, therefore, this silver revolution in the period *circa* 1520 to *circa* 1680.[1]

Where did the silver come from? Current opinion is that it must have come from internal sources; it was unlikely to have come from abroad. While admitting that some may have come from internal sources, from precious metals previously used for non-monetary purposes, it must also be admitted that it could have come from abroad. Certainly the arguments currently used to refute this suggestion do not constitute a very convincing case. The statistics and other sources commonly used to suggest a perhaps chronically unfavourable trade balance can be criticised on a number of grounds. Some, for example, relate to particular years, not to long periods. Often they were drawn up for a particular purpose; sometimes to support schemes which were regulatory or restrictive in intent.[2] While Professor Fisher's series are less prone to this sort of objection, too-sweeping conclusions have been drawn, not always by him, from what are after all figures of woollen cloth exports from London. Also far too little attention has been paid to the balance of payments rather than the balance of trade. Developments such as the growing proportion of goods carried in English ships, and increasing native participation in marine insurance must have worked to improve the payments position. Interest payments on debts contracted with foreigners may have constituted a drain in the period

---

Watson, 'Back to Gold – and Silver', *Economic History Review*, 2nd series, XX (1967), 1–58. He shows how in the early Middle Ages Europe experienced shortages of gold but an abundance of silver, while the Muslim world enjoyed plenty of gold but little silver, how also this position was reversed from the mid-thirteenth century, and how these various experiences were closely interrelated.

[1] These observations are all based on a scrutiny of the figures in Appendix I of Craig, *op. cit.*, pp. 408–22.

[2] Professor Stone's sources are particularly susceptible to this sort of criticism. Contemporary complaints about unfavourable balances also owe much to special pleading for lucrative regulatory offices.

1544–72, but thereafter presented little or no problem.[1] Practically no work has been done on capital movements: some items probably resulted in net gains, the ending of Papal dues, immigrant funds; others were periodically negative, such as subsidies to allies, and the payments for English troops operating abroad. On the whole there are far too many unknowns for us to pronounce that the balance of payments was persistently negative, and it is unlikely that the occasionally heavy capital outflows of the Elizabethan period could have been effected without positive balances being earned elsewhere.[2]

The whole question of specie flows is as yet uncharted territory, and especially shameful is the neglect of this subject in the period of the great debasement. The latter could have resulted in a considerable flow of precious metals to this country, especially of silver. A number of mechanisms deserve careful investigation. One is the effect of debasement on trade. Brenner, for example, acknowledges that there was a rapid increase in English exports, but states that there was also a corresponding increase in imports, so that the net effect on the balance of trade was slight.[3] At another point, he draws heavily on Professor Supple to show that the enhancement of monies in English export markets abroad could lead to serious specie drains from this country.[4] It is difficult to see why heavy enhancement and debasement in this country did not lead to some inflows of specie, since the mechanism was

[1] R. B. Outhwaite, 'The Trials of Foreign Borrowing: The English Crown and the Antwerp Money Market in the Mid-Sixteenth Century', *Economic History Review*, 2nd series, XIX (1966), 289–305.

[2] Including capital gains derived from privateering. The return from Drake's expedition of 1577–80 was estimated at a million and a half sterling, of which perhaps £600,000 was in specie: W. R. Scott, *The Constitution and Finance of English, Scottish and Irish Joint-Stock Companies to 1720* (3 vols., Cambridge, 1912), I, 78–85. Although this was probably the most spectacularly successful of such ventures, unsuccessful ones did not represent a very considerable external loss since most payments were made in England, for outfitting, provisioning, etc., before sailing, and rewards, if any, were distributed on return. Purchases from foreigners would thus be very small.

[3] Brenner, *Econ. Hist. Rev.*, 1961, p. 228. He cites Professor Fisher for support, but Fisher was circumspect and hedged this conclusion with considerable qualifications: see F. J. Fisher, 'Commercial Trends and Policy', pp. 99–101.

[4] Brenner, *Econ. Hist. Rev.*, 1962, pp. 274–5.

similar in both cases.[1] Secondly, the debasement of the coinage was likely to result in specie flows independent of movements in trade. The heavy debasement of both metals could result in both gold and silver entering this country, because of the higher nominal returns to be gained.[2] It it possible that this happened, though the subject is largely uninvestigated. If one metal was debased more than the other, there would be a tendency for bi-metallic flows to be encouraged, with the most debased metal entering the country and the least leaving it. This almost certainly happened. In the early sixteenth century there was a tendency for gold to be undervalued in terms of silver, gold was thus exported. The alterations of 1526 slightly reduced this undervaluation but not enough to really effect an improvement.[3] Although both metals suffered in the great debasement following 1542, silver suffered much more than gold, with the result that the ratio dropped from 12.3 to 1 in 1541 by steps to a ridiculous 5 to 1 by 1546, a ratio which grossly undervalued gold.[4] It was not until 1551 that a step was taken in the right direction with the restoration of a ratio of about 11 to 1, and in 1560 with one of about 12 to 1.[5] There was a persistent tendency in the sixteenth century, however, for gold to be undervalued in terms of silver. We should expect, therefore, gold to leave this country and silver to enter it, a bimetallic flow that should have been enormously accelerated during the period of the great debasement. That the latter actually occurred is amply suggested in monetary expert, William Lane's letter to Cecil, written in 1551, in the depths of the great debasement. The 'lightness' of the silver coin had resulted in a great fall of the exchange and was causing merchants to export gold 'for that hyt ys to a more profyt than the exchange.

[1] Merchants would find it difficult to sell imported goods for which any English substitutes existed, and would find it easier to export goods from England, since in both cases the prices of native goods rose much more slowly than the external value of the currency fell. The process is admirably explained in B. E. Supple, *Commercial Crisis and Change in England, 1600–1642* (Cambridge, 1959), pp. 73–5.

[2] Either legally through coining, because a given weight of metal would purchase more, or illegally by way of counterfeit coins. There is plenty of evidence to suggest that the latter was a problem.

[3] Oman, *op. cit.*, pp. 248–52. The ratio moved from about 12 to 1 to about 12.3 to 1.

[4] *Ibid.*, p. 256.   [5] *Ibid.*, pp. 268, 278.

And the lyke of thys myscheffe hapnyd here in ynglo[n]d in the
monthes of June, Julii, and awguste laste, in the wyche 3 monthes
was caryyd owte of ynglond not so lyttyll as a hundarthe
thowsand powndes of gold; and yette dyd there sylvar cume in to
the land as faste, and all for the private gayne in quyngnge the
sylvar styll, and also was carryd awaye, for that the pownd of gold
ys Rychar than the pownd of whyte mony, . . . so that shortely we
schall be quite off all owre Ryche mony for a base quyne . . .'[1]
The readjustment of the Mint price in 1551, and the trade
depressions which ensued, halted and may temporarily have
reversed, the inward flow of specie. This probably lay behind the
re-enactment in 1553 of the Act forbidding the export of specie,[2]
which had significantly been in abeyance since 1509. It is unlikely,
however, that the halting of debasement resulted in any
permanent end to this bimetallic flow, which probably continued
into the later sixteenth century.[3] The argument is, then, that
debasement may have induced inward flows of both metals, but
that it almost certainly resulted in a massive inflow of silver, an
inflow which may have slackened, but probably did not disappear,
when debasement ended. Inward flows of both metals would
obviously cause an increase in the precious metal stock, but the
effects on circulation of the mere substitution of one metal for
another are more mysterious. Some people have argued that this
would increase the velocity of circulation, since silver coin – the
'pale and common drudge 'tween man and man' – had a greater
velocity than gold. This may well be true, but one further possibility deserves consideration. This is that the gold which was
exported was not necessarily monetised gold; the undervaluation
of gold would make it profitable to melt down gold plate, jewelry
and other ornaments. The fact that gold was relatively abundant
in England in the later Middle Ages must have resulted in a
considerable non-monetary stock of gold.[4] Did this slowly disappear in the course of the sixteenth century? Whatever the

[1] Tawney and Power, *op. cit.*, II, 182–6. Gresham also, of course,
drew attention to this external drain of gold: see his famous letter to
Elizabeth on the fall of the exchanges, *ibid.*, II, 146–9.

[2] *Ibid.*, II, 177–8.

[3] Cunningham, *The Growth of English Industry and Commerce*
(Cambridge, 5th ed., 1922), I, 137–9.

[4] Cunningham commented on 'extraordinary and extravagant' non-
monetary uses of precious metals in England in the later Middle Ages

answer to questions such as this, the possibility of specie, and especially bimetallic, flows accounting for this silver revolution cannot be lightly dismissed.

It is not possible in a survey such as this to tie up all the loose ends, to answer all the questions that need answering. Indeed it must be clear that much work needs to be undertaken before we can conclusively do so. The task of this author has been to present the reader with what men, past and present, have thought and written about the subject and to explore the weaknesses of their various explanations. It is hoped that the issues, at least, are a little clearer.

(*ibid.*, p. 545). Not all of course consisted of gold, nor was all of it subsequently exported. There would be strong pressures, especially in the first half of the sixteenth century, to mint such metals since for long periods the value of coined money was greater than that of precious metals. This was probably the most important force resulting in dehoarding of such stocks. Other elements, such as the sack of the monasteries, still await careful investigation.

Select Bibliography

Since this study is an extended bibliographical commentary attention is here confined to the more important of recent works on this subject. Additional bibliographical comment will be found in the footnotes. The place of publication is London, unless otherwise stated.

E. H. Phelps Brown and Sheila V. Hopkins, 'Seven Centuries of Building Wages', *Economica*, XXII (1955), 195–206; 'Seven Centuries of the Prices of Consumables, compared with Builders' Wage-rates', *ibid.*, XXIII (1956), 296–314 (both articles are reprinted in E. Carus Wilson (ed.), *Essays in Economic History* (London, 1962), vol. II, 168–96); 'Wage-rates and Prices: Evidence for Population Pressure in the Sixteenth Century', *Economica*, XXIV (1957), 289–306; 'Builders' Wage-rates, Prices and Population: Some Further Evidence', *ibid.*, XXVI (1959), 18–38. An influential reworking of mainly old price series, undertaken with more skill and caution than their critics sometimes suggest.

I. Hammarström, 'The "Price Revolution" of the Sixteenth Century: Some Swedish Evidence', *Scandinavian Economic History Review*, V, no. 2 (1957), 118–54. More wide-ranging than its title implies. The best introduction to the problems of this subject.

Y. S. Brenner, 'The Inflation of Prices in Early Sixteenth Century England', *Econ. Hist. Rev.*, 2nd series, XIV, no. 2 (1961), 225–39; 'The Inflation of Prices in England, 1551–1650', *ibid.*, XV, no. 2 (1962), 266–84. The only modern sustained discussion of the English price rise, but slapdash and often obscure.

J. D. Gould, 'Y. S. Brenner on Prices: A Comment', *Econ. Hist. Rev.*, XVI, no. 2 (1963), 351–60; 'The Price Revolution Reconsidered', *ibid.*, XVII, no. 2 (1964), 249–66. Mingles intelligent criticism with positive suggestions of sometimes dubious value.

56

Geoffrey Maynard, *Economic Development and the Price Level* (London, 1962). An economist looks at historical experience of inflation.

P. Bowden, 'Agricultural Prices, Farm Profits, and Rents', in Joan Thirsk (ed.), *The Agrarian History of England and Wales*, vol. IV, *1500–1640* (Cambridge, 1967), pp. 593–695. An interesting 'physical' interpretation of the trends and fluctuations in agricultural product prices in this period.

F. P. Braudel and F. Spooner, 'Prices in Europe from 1450 to 1750' in E. E. Rich and C. H. Wilson (eds.), *The Cambridge Economic History of Europe*, vol. IV (Cambridge, 1967), pp. 378–486. Selective and discursive, and ultimately inconclusive, but contains also insights of value to the advanced student.

Index